The Gourmet Pizza Kitchen: 50 Recipes

By: Kelly Johnson

Table of Contents

- Margherita Pizza
- Classic Pepperoni Pizza
- Four Cheese Pizza
- BBQ Chicken Pizza
- Mediterranean Veggie Pizza
- Hawaiian Pizza
- Spinach and Feta Pizza
- Buffalo Chicken Pizza
- Meat Lover's Pizza
- Pesto Chicken Pizza
- Truffle Mushroom Pizza
- Caprese Pizza
- Prosciutto and Arugula Pizza
- White Garlic Sauce Pizza
- Sausage and Peppers Pizza
- Shrimp Scampi Pizza
- Smoked Salmon and Dill Pizza
- Spicy Jalapeño and Bacon Pizza
- Vegan Margherita Pizza
- Sweet Potato and Goat Cheese Pizza
- Thai Chicken Pizza
- BBQ Pulled Pork Pizza
- Cheeseburger Pizza
- Taco Pizza
- Philly Cheesesteak Pizza
- Roasted Veggie and Hummus Pizza
- Artichoke and Olive Pizza
- Eggplant Parmesan Pizza
- Balsamic Glazed Fig and Prosciutto Pizza
- Pear and Gorgonzola Pizza
- Chicken Alfredo Pizza
- Zucchini and Ricotta Pizza
- Smoked Gouda and Bacon Pizza
- Pineapple and Jalapeño Pizza
- Roasted Garlic and Spinach Pizza

- Clam and Bacon Pizza
- Breakfast Pizza with Eggs and Bacon
- Spicy Chorizo Pizza
- Butternut Squash and Sage Pizza
- Lobster and Brie Pizza
- Spicy Honey and Pepperoni Pizza
- Cauliflower Crust Pizza
- Rustic Ratatouille Pizza
- Avocado and Egg Pizza
- Kimchi and Pork Belly Pizza
- Pulled Duck and Hoisin Sauce Pizza
- Pumpkin and Feta Pizza
- Heirloom Tomato and Basil Pizza
- Mac and Cheese Pizza
- Dark Chocolate and Strawberry Dessert Pizza

Margherita Pizza

Ingredients:

- 1 pizza dough
- 1/2 cup pizza sauce
- 8 oz fresh mozzarella, sliced
- Fresh basil leaves
- 1 tbsp olive oil
- Salt to taste

Instructions:

1. Preheat the oven to 475°F (245°C).
2. Roll out pizza dough and spread pizza sauce evenly.
3. Top with mozzarella slices and bake for 10-12 minutes.
4. Add fresh basil leaves and drizzle with olive oil before serving.

Classic Pepperoni Pizza

Ingredients:

- 1 pizza dough
- 1/2 cup pizza sauce
- 1 cup shredded mozzarella cheese
- 20-25 slices of pepperoni

Instructions:

1. Preheat the oven to 475°F (245°C).
2. Spread pizza sauce over the rolled-out dough.
3. Sprinkle with mozzarella and arrange pepperoni slices on top.
4. Bake for 12-15 minutes, or until the crust is golden.

Four Cheese Pizza

Ingredients:

- 1 pizza dough
- 1/2 cup pizza sauce
- 1/4 cup mozzarella cheese
- 1/4 cup provolone cheese
- 1/4 cup Parmesan cheese
- 1/4 cup ricotta cheese

Instructions:

1. Preheat the oven to 475°F (245°C).
2. Spread sauce on the pizza dough and layer with mozzarella, provolone, Parmesan, and dollops of ricotta.
3. Bake for 12-15 minutes, until cheeses are melted and bubbly.

BBQ Chicken Pizza

Ingredients:

- 1 pizza dough
- 1/2 cup BBQ sauce
- 1 cup cooked chicken, shredded
- 1/2 cup red onion, sliced
- 1 cup shredded mozzarella cheese
- Fresh cilantro for garnish

Instructions:

1. Preheat the oven to 475°F (245°C).
2. Spread BBQ sauce on the pizza dough.
3. Top with chicken, onion, and mozzarella.
4. Bake for 12-15 minutes and garnish with cilantro before serving.

Mediterranean Veggie Pizza

Ingredients:

- 1 pizza dough
- 1/2 cup pizza sauce
- 1/4 cup sliced black olives
- 1/4 cup chopped artichokes
- 1/4 cup crumbled feta cheese
- 1/2 cup shredded mozzarella
- 1/2 cup cherry tomatoes, halved

Instructions:

1. Preheat the oven to 475°F (245°C).
2. Spread sauce on the dough and layer with olives, artichokes, feta, mozzarella, and tomatoes.
3. Bake for 12-15 minutes.

Hawaiian Pizza

Ingredients:

- 1 pizza dough
- 1/2 cup pizza sauce
- 1 cup shredded mozzarella
- 1/2 cup ham, diced
- 1/2 cup pineapple chunks

Instructions:

1. Preheat the oven to 475°F (245°C).
2. Spread sauce on the pizza dough and top with mozzarella, ham, and pineapple.
3. Bake for 12-15 minutes.

Spinach and Feta Pizza

Ingredients:

- 1 pizza dough
- 1/2 cup Alfredo sauce
- 1 cup fresh spinach leaves
- 1/4 cup crumbled feta cheese
- 1 cup shredded mozzarella cheese

Instructions:

1. Preheat the oven to 475°F (245°C).
2. Spread Alfredo sauce over the dough.
3. Top with spinach, feta, and mozzarella.
4. Bake for 12-15 minutes.

Buffalo Chicken Pizza

Ingredients:

- 1 pizza dough
- 1/4 cup buffalo sauce
- 1 cup cooked chicken, shredded
- 1/2 cup shredded mozzarella cheese
- 1/2 cup blue cheese crumbles

Instructions:

1. Preheat the oven to 475°F (245°C).
2. Spread buffalo sauce on the pizza dough and top with chicken, mozzarella, and blue cheese.
3. Bake for 12-15 minutes.

Meat Lover's Pizza

Ingredients:

- 1 pizza dough
- 1/2 cup pizza sauce
- 1 cup shredded mozzarella cheese
- 1/2 cup cooked sausage, crumbled
- 1/4 cup pepperoni slices
- 1/4 cup diced ham
- 1/4 cup cooked bacon bits

Instructions:

1. Preheat the oven to 475°F (245°C).
2. Spread pizza sauce on the dough and sprinkle with mozzarella.
3. Layer sausage, pepperoni, ham, and bacon evenly.
4. Bake for 12-15 minutes.

Pesto Chicken Pizza

Ingredients:

- 1 pizza dough
- 1/2 cup pesto sauce
- 1 cup shredded cooked chicken
- 1/2 cup shredded mozzarella cheese
- 1/4 cup cherry tomatoes, halved
- 2 tbsp grated Parmesan cheese

Instructions:

1. Preheat the oven to 475°F (245°C).
2. Spread pesto over the dough and top with chicken, mozzarella, and tomatoes.
3. Sprinkle with Parmesan and bake for 12-15 minutes.

Truffle Mushroom Pizza

Ingredients:

- 1 pizza dough
- 1/2 cup Alfredo sauce
- 1 cup mushrooms, thinly sliced
- 1 cup shredded mozzarella cheese
- 1 tbsp truffle oil
- Fresh thyme leaves for garnish

Instructions:

1. Preheat the oven to 475°F (245°C).
2. Spread Alfredo sauce on the dough and top with mushrooms and mozzarella.
3. Drizzle with truffle oil and bake for 12-15 minutes. Garnish with thyme.

Caprese Pizza

Ingredients:

- 1 pizza dough
- 1/2 cup pizza sauce
- 8 oz fresh mozzarella, sliced
- 1/2 cup cherry tomatoes, halved
- Fresh basil leaves
- 1 tbsp balsamic glaze

Instructions:

1. Preheat the oven to 475°F (245°C).
2. Spread pizza sauce on the dough and layer with mozzarella and cherry tomatoes.
3. Bake for 10-12 minutes. Add basil and drizzle with balsamic glaze before serving.

Prosciutto and Arugula Pizza

Ingredients:

- 1 pizza dough
- 1/2 cup Alfredo sauce
- 1 cup shredded mozzarella cheese
- 4 slices prosciutto
- 1 cup fresh arugula
- 1 tbsp olive oil
- Shaved Parmesan for garnish

Instructions:

1. Preheat the oven to 475°F (245°C).
2. Spread Alfredo sauce on the dough and sprinkle with mozzarella.
3. Bake for 10-12 minutes. Top with prosciutto, arugula, olive oil, and Parmesan before serving.

White Garlic Sauce Pizza

Ingredients:

- 1 pizza dough
- 1/2 cup garlic Alfredo sauce
- 1 cup shredded mozzarella cheese
- 1/2 cup ricotta cheese, dolloped
- 1/2 cup Parmesan cheese
- Fresh parsley for garnish

Instructions:

1. Preheat the oven to 475°F (245°C).
2. Spread garlic Alfredo sauce on the dough.
3. Layer mozzarella, ricotta dollops, and Parmesan.
4. Bake for 12-15 minutes and garnish with parsley.

Sausage and Peppers Pizza

Ingredients:

- 1 pizza dough
- 1/2 cup pizza sauce
- 1 cup cooked sausage, crumbled
- 1/2 cup bell peppers, sliced
- 1 cup shredded mozzarella cheese

Instructions:

1. Preheat the oven to 475°F (245°C).
2. Spread pizza sauce on the dough and layer sausage, peppers, and mozzarella.
3. Bake for 12-15 minutes.

Shrimp Scampi Pizza

Ingredients:

- 1 pizza dough
- 1/2 cup garlic butter sauce
- 1 cup cooked shrimp
- 1/2 cup shredded mozzarella cheese
- 2 tbsp grated Parmesan cheese
- 1 tbsp chopped parsley

Instructions:

1. Preheat the oven to 475°F (245°C).
2. Spread garlic butter sauce on the dough and top with shrimp, mozzarella, and Parmesan.
3. Bake for 12-15 minutes. Garnish with parsley before serving.

Smoked Salmon and Dill Pizza

Ingredients:

- 1 pizza dough
- 1/2 cup crème fraîche or cream cheese
- 4 oz smoked salmon, thinly sliced
- 1 tbsp fresh dill, chopped
- 1 tbsp capers
- 1/4 cup thinly sliced red onion

Instructions:

1. Preheat the oven to 475°F (245°C).
2. Bake the pizza dough until golden and let it cool slightly.
3. Spread crème fraîche on the dough and layer with smoked salmon, red onion, capers, and dill.

Spicy Jalapeño and Bacon Pizza

Ingredients:

- 1 pizza dough
- 1/2 cup pizza sauce
- 1 cup shredded mozzarella cheese
- 1/4 cup pickled jalapeños, sliced
- 4 strips bacon, cooked and crumbled
- 1/4 tsp crushed red pepper flakes

Instructions:

1. Preheat the oven to 475°F (245°C).
2. Spread pizza sauce on the dough and sprinkle with mozzarella.
3. Add jalapeños, bacon, and red pepper flakes.
4. Bake for 12-15 minutes.

Vegan Margherita Pizza

Ingredients:

- 1 pizza dough
- 1/2 cup tomato sauce
- 8 oz vegan mozzarella, sliced
- Fresh basil leaves
- 1 tbsp olive oil

Instructions:

1. Preheat the oven to 475°F (245°C).
2. Spread tomato sauce on the dough and top with vegan mozzarella.
3. Bake for 10-12 minutes. Add fresh basil and drizzle with olive oil before serving.

Sweet Potato and Goat Cheese Pizza

Ingredients:

- 1 pizza dough
- 1/2 cup Alfredo sauce
- 1 medium sweet potato, thinly sliced and roasted
- 1/4 cup crumbled goat cheese
- 1 tbsp honey
- Fresh thyme leaves

Instructions:

1. Preheat the oven to 475°F (245°C).
2. Spread Alfredo sauce on the dough and layer with roasted sweet potato and goat cheese.
3. Bake for 12-15 minutes. Drizzle with honey and garnish with thyme before serving.

Thai Chicken Pizza

Ingredients:

- 1 pizza dough
- 1/2 cup peanut sauce
- 1 cup cooked chicken, shredded
- 1/2 cup shredded carrots
- 1/4 cup chopped peanuts
- 1 tbsp chopped cilantro

Instructions:

1. Preheat the oven to 475°F (245°C).
2. Spread peanut sauce on the dough and top with chicken, carrots, and mozzarella.
3. Bake for 12-15 minutes. Garnish with chopped peanuts and cilantro.

BBQ Pulled Pork Pizza

Ingredients:

- 1 pizza dough
- 1/2 cup BBQ sauce
- 1 cup shredded pulled pork
- 1/4 cup red onion, thinly sliced
- 1 cup shredded mozzarella cheese
- 1/4 cup chopped fresh cilantro

Instructions:

1. Preheat the oven to 475°F (245°C).
2. Spread BBQ sauce on the dough and layer with pulled pork, red onion, and mozzarella.
3. Bake for 12-15 minutes. Sprinkle cilantro on top before serving.

Cheeseburger Pizza

Ingredients:

- 1 pizza dough
- 1/2 cup ketchup and mustard mixture (2:1 ratio)
- 1 cup cooked ground beef
- 1/2 cup shredded cheddar cheese
- 1/4 cup diced pickles
- 1/4 cup diced tomatoes
- Shredded lettuce for topping

Instructions:

1. Preheat the oven to 475°F (245°C).
2. Spread the ketchup-mustard mixture on the dough.
3. Add ground beef, cheddar, and bake for 12-15 minutes.
4. Top with pickles, tomatoes, and shredded lettuce before serving.

Taco Pizza

Ingredients:

- 1 pizza dough
- 1/2 cup salsa
- 1 cup cooked ground taco-seasoned beef or beans
- 1 cup shredded cheddar cheese
- 1/2 cup shredded lettuce
- 1/4 cup diced tomatoes
- 1/4 cup sliced black olives
- Sour cream for garnish

Instructions:

1. Preheat the oven to 475°F (245°C).
2. Spread salsa on the dough and top with taco-seasoned beef and cheese.
3. Bake for 12-15 minutes. Add lettuce, tomatoes, and olives after baking. Drizzle with sour cream before serving.

Philly Cheesesteak Pizza

Ingredients:

- 1 pizza dough
- 1/2 cup pizza sauce
- 1 cup cooked steak, thinly sliced
- 1/2 cup sautéed bell peppers, sliced
- 1/2 cup sautéed onions, sliced
- 1 cup shredded provolone cheese
- 1/4 cup shredded mozzarella cheese

Instructions:

1. Preheat the oven to 475°F (245°C).
2. Spread pizza sauce on the dough and top with steak, bell peppers, onions, and cheeses.
3. Bake for 12-15 minutes until the cheese is melted and bubbly.

Roasted Veggie and Hummus Pizza

Ingredients:

- 1 pizza dough
- 1/2 cup hummus (any flavor you prefer)
- 1 cup mixed roasted veggies (zucchini, bell peppers, onions, mushrooms)
- 1/2 cup crumbled feta cheese
- Fresh parsley for garnish

Instructions:

1. Preheat the oven to 475°F (245°C).
2. Spread hummus on the dough and top with roasted veggies and feta.
3. Bake for 10-12 minutes. Garnish with fresh parsley before serving.

Artichoke and Olive Pizza

Ingredients:

- 1 pizza dough
- 1/2 cup pesto sauce
- 1 cup canned artichoke hearts, drained and chopped
- 1/4 cup Kalamata olives, sliced
- 1 cup shredded mozzarella cheese
- 1/4 cup grated Parmesan cheese

Instructions:

1. Preheat the oven to 475°F (245°C).
2. Spread pesto sauce on the dough and top with artichokes, olives, mozzarella, and Parmesan.
3. Bake for 12-15 minutes until golden and bubbly.

Eggplant Parmesan Pizza

Ingredients:

- 1 pizza dough
- 1/2 cup marinara sauce
- 1 medium eggplant, sliced and roasted
- 1 cup shredded mozzarella cheese
- 1/4 cup grated Parmesan cheese
- Fresh basil leaves

Instructions:

1. Preheat the oven to 475°F (245°C).
2. Spread marinara sauce on the dough and layer with roasted eggplant, mozzarella, and Parmesan.
3. Bake for 12-15 minutes. Garnish with fresh basil before serving.

Balsamic Glazed Fig and Prosciutto Pizza

Ingredients:

- 1 pizza dough
- 1/2 cup goat cheese or ricotta
- 1/2 cup figs, sliced
- 4 slices prosciutto
- 1 tbsp balsamic glaze
- Fresh arugula for garnish

Instructions:

1. Preheat the oven to 475°F (245°C).
2. Spread goat cheese on the dough and top with figs and prosciutto.
3. Bake for 12-15 minutes. Drizzle with balsamic glaze and garnish with arugula before serving.

Pear and Gorgonzola Pizza

Ingredients:

- 1 pizza dough
- 1/2 cup crème fraîche or ricotta
- 1 pear, thinly sliced
- 1/4 cup crumbled Gorgonzola cheese
- 1 tbsp honey
- Fresh thyme leaves

Instructions:

1. Preheat the oven to 475°F (245°C).
2. Spread crème fraîche on the dough and layer with pear slices and Gorgonzola.
3. Bake for 10-12 minutes. Drizzle with honey and sprinkle with thyme before serving.

Chicken Alfredo Pizza

Ingredients:

- 1 pizza dough
- 1/2 cup Alfredo sauce
- 1 cup cooked chicken, shredded
- 1 cup shredded mozzarella cheese
- 1/4 cup grated Parmesan cheese
- Fresh parsley for garnish

Instructions:

1. Preheat the oven to 475°F (245°C).
2. Spread Alfredo sauce on the dough and top with chicken and cheeses.
3. Bake for 12-15 minutes. Garnish with fresh parsley before serving.

Zucchini and Ricotta Pizza

Ingredients:

- 1 pizza dough
- 1/2 cup ricotta cheese
- 1 zucchini, thinly sliced
- 1 cup shredded mozzarella cheese
- 1 tbsp olive oil
- Fresh basil for garnish

Instructions:

1. Preheat the oven to 475°F (245°C).
2. Spread ricotta cheese on the dough and layer with zucchini slices and mozzarella.
3. Drizzle with olive oil and bake for 12-15 minutes. Garnish with fresh basil before serving.

Smoked Gouda and Bacon Pizza

Ingredients:

- 1 pizza dough
- 1/2 cup Alfredo sauce
- 1 cup shredded smoked Gouda cheese
- 4 strips bacon, cooked and crumbled
- 1/4 cup caramelized onions
- Fresh parsley for garnish

Instructions:

1. Preheat the oven to 475°F (245°C).
2. Spread Alfredo sauce on the dough and top with smoked Gouda, bacon, and caramelized onions.
3. Bake for 12-15 minutes. Garnish with fresh parsley before serving.

Pineapple and Jalapeño Pizza

Ingredients:

- 1 pizza dough
- 1/2 cup pizza sauce
- 1 cup shredded mozzarella cheese
- 1/2 cup pineapple chunks
- 1/4 cup sliced jalapeños
- 1/4 cup red onion, thinly sliced

Instructions:

1. Preheat the oven to 475°F (245°C).
2. Spread pizza sauce on the dough and top with mozzarella, pineapple, jalapeños, and red onion.
3. Bake for 12-15 minutes until the cheese is melted and bubbly.

Roasted Garlic and Spinach Pizza

Ingredients:

- 1 pizza dough
- 1/2 cup olive oil
- 5 cloves garlic, minced
- 2 cups fresh spinach, wilted
- 1 cup shredded mozzarella cheese
- 1/4 cup grated Parmesan cheese
- 1/4 tsp crushed red pepper flakes

Instructions:

1. Preheat the oven to 475°F (245°C).
2. Heat olive oil in a pan and sauté garlic until fragrant, then spread the oil and garlic over the pizza dough.
3. Top with wilted spinach, mozzarella, and Parmesan.
4. Bake for 12-15 minutes. Garnish with crushed red pepper flakes before serving.

Clam and Bacon Pizza

Ingredients:

- 1 pizza dough
- 1/2 cup white wine sauce or Alfredo sauce
- 1 cup cooked clams, drained
- 4 strips bacon, cooked and crumbled
- 1/2 cup shredded mozzarella cheese
- Fresh parsley for garnish

Instructions:

1. Preheat the oven to 475°F (245°C).
2. Spread white wine sauce over the dough and layer with clams, bacon, and mozzarella.
3. Bake for 12-15 minutes. Garnish with fresh parsley before serving.

Breakfast Pizza with Eggs and Bacon

Ingredients:

- 1 pizza dough
- 1/2 cup pizza sauce or olive oil
- 1 cup shredded mozzarella cheese
- 4 strips cooked bacon, crumbled
- 2 eggs
- Fresh chives for garnish

Instructions:

1. Preheat the oven to 475°F (245°C).
2. Spread pizza sauce or olive oil over the dough, then top with mozzarella, bacon, and a space for each egg.
3. Crack the eggs onto the pizza and bake for 12-15 minutes, until the eggs are cooked to your liking.
4. Garnish with fresh chives before serving.

Spicy Chorizo Pizza

Ingredients:

- 1 pizza dough
- 1/2 cup tomato sauce
- 1 cup shredded mozzarella cheese
- 1/2 cup crumbled spicy chorizo sausage
- 1/4 cup sliced red onion
- 1/4 cup chopped cilantro

Instructions:

1. Preheat the oven to 475°F (245°C).
2. Spread tomato sauce on the dough and top with mozzarella, chorizo, and red onion.
3. Bake for 12-15 minutes. Garnish with cilantro before serving.

Butternut Squash and Sage Pizza

Ingredients:

- 1 pizza dough
- 1/2 cup olive oil
- 1 cup roasted butternut squash, mashed
- 1/4 cup crumbled goat cheese or ricotta
- 1/4 cup fresh sage leaves
- 1/4 cup grated Parmesan cheese

Instructions:

1. Preheat the oven to 475°F (245°C).
2. Spread olive oil on the dough and top with mashed butternut squash, goat cheese, and fresh sage.
3. Bake for 12-15 minutes. Sprinkle with Parmesan before serving.

Lobster and Brie Pizza

Ingredients:

- 1 pizza dough
- 1/2 cup Alfredo sauce
- 1/2 cup cooked lobster meat, chopped
- 1/2 cup Brie cheese, sliced
- 1/4 cup fresh chives, chopped
- 1/4 tsp lemon zest

Instructions:

1. Preheat the oven to 475°F (245°C).
2. Spread Alfredo sauce on the dough and top with lobster, Brie, and chives.
3. Bake for 12-15 minutes. Garnish with lemon zest before serving.

Spicy Honey and Pepperoni Pizza

Ingredients:

- 1 pizza dough
- 1/2 cup pizza sauce
- 1 cup shredded mozzarella cheese
- 1/2 cup sliced pepperoni
- 1 tbsp spicy honey (or regular honey with a pinch of chili flakes)
- Fresh basil for garnish

Instructions:

1. Preheat the oven to 475°F (245°C).
2. Spread pizza sauce on the dough and top with mozzarella and pepperoni.
3. Bake for 12-15 minutes. Drizzle with spicy honey and garnish with basil before serving.

Cauliflower Crust Pizza

Ingredients:

- 1 cauliflower head (riced)
- 1 cup shredded mozzarella cheese
- 1/4 cup grated Parmesan cheese
- 1 egg
- 1 tsp garlic powder
- 1 tsp dried oregano
- 1/4 tsp salt
- 1/4 tsp black pepper
- Your favorite pizza toppings (tomato sauce, mozzarella, veggies, etc.)

Instructions:

1. Preheat the oven to 425°F (220°C).
2. Rice the cauliflower by pulsing it in a food processor until it resembles rice.
3. Microwave the cauliflower for 5-7 minutes, then cool it and squeeze out excess moisture using a clean towel.
4. In a bowl, mix the cauliflower with mozzarella, Parmesan, egg, garlic powder, oregano, salt, and pepper.
5. Shape the mixture into a crust on a parchment-lined baking sheet.
6. Bake for 12-15 minutes until golden and crisp.
7. Top with your favorite pizza toppings and bake for another 5-7 minutes.

Rustic Ratatouille Pizza

Ingredients:

- 1 pizza dough
- 1/2 cup tomato sauce
- 1 small eggplant, thinly sliced
- 1 zucchini, thinly sliced
- 1 bell pepper, thinly sliced
- 1 small onion, thinly sliced
- 1/2 cup shredded mozzarella cheese
- 1/4 tsp dried thyme
- 1/4 tsp dried oregano
- Fresh basil for garnish

Instructions:

1. Preheat the oven to 475°F (245°C).
2. Spread tomato sauce on the pizza dough.
3. Arrange the eggplant, zucchini, bell pepper, and onion on top.
4. Sprinkle with mozzarella, thyme, and oregano.
5. Bake for 12-15 minutes. Garnish with fresh basil before serving.

Avocado and Egg Pizza

Ingredients:

- 1 pizza dough
- 1/2 cup pizza sauce or olive oil
- 1 cup shredded mozzarella cheese
- 1 ripe avocado, sliced
- 2 eggs
- 1/4 tsp crushed red pepper flakes
- Fresh cilantro for garnish

Instructions:

1. Preheat the oven to 475°F (245°C).
2. Spread pizza sauce or olive oil on the dough. Top with mozzarella and sliced avocado.
3. Crack two eggs onto the pizza, leaving space between them.
4. Bake for 12-15 minutes, until the eggs are cooked to your liking.
5. Garnish with crushed red pepper flakes and fresh cilantro before serving.

Kimchi and Pork Belly Pizza

Ingredients:

- 1 pizza dough
- 1/2 cup gochujang (Korean chili paste)
- 1 cup shredded mozzarella cheese
- 1/2 cup kimchi, chopped
- 1/2 cup cooked pork belly, sliced
- 1/4 cup green onions, chopped
- Sesame seeds for garnish

Instructions:

1. Preheat the oven to 475°F (245°C).
2. Spread gochujang on the pizza dough as the base sauce.
3. Top with mozzarella, kimchi, pork belly, and green onions.
4. Bake for 12-15 minutes. Garnish with sesame seeds before serving.

Pulled Duck and Hoisin Sauce Pizza

Ingredients:

- 1 pizza dough
- 1/4 cup hoisin sauce
- 1 cup shredded mozzarella cheese
- 1/2 cup pulled duck meat
- 1/4 cup sliced red onion
- Fresh cilantro for garnish
- Sriracha sauce for drizzle

Instructions:

1. Preheat the oven to 475°F (245°C).
2. Spread hoisin sauce on the pizza dough.
3. Top with mozzarella, pulled duck, and red onion.
4. Bake for 12-15 minutes. Garnish with fresh cilantro and drizzle with Sriracha sauce before serving.

Pumpkin and Feta Pizza

Ingredients:

- 1 pizza dough
- 1/2 cup olive oil
- 1 cup canned pumpkin puree
- 1/4 tsp cinnamon
- 1/4 tsp nutmeg
- 1 cup crumbled feta cheese
- 1/4 cup roasted pumpkin seeds
- Fresh sage leaves for garnish

Instructions:

1. Preheat the oven to 475°F (245°C).
2. Spread olive oil on the dough, then top with pumpkin puree.
3. Sprinkle cinnamon and nutmeg over the pumpkin, followed by feta cheese and pumpkin seeds.
4. Bake for 12-15 minutes. Garnish with fresh sage before serving.

Heirloom Tomato and Basil Pizza

Ingredients:

- 1 pizza dough
- 1/2 cup tomato sauce
- 2 heirloom tomatoes, sliced
- 1 cup fresh mozzarella cheese, torn
- 1/4 cup fresh basil leaves
- Olive oil for drizzling

Instructions:

1. Preheat the oven to 475°F (245°C).
2. Spread tomato sauce on the pizza dough, then arrange heirloom tomatoes and mozzarella on top.
3. Bake for 12-15 minutes, until cheese is melted.
4. Garnish with fresh basil and drizzle with olive oil before serving.

Mac and Cheese Pizza

Ingredients:

- 1 pizza dough
- 1/2 cup cheddar cheese sauce (prepared)
- 1 cup cooked macaroni pasta
- 1 cup shredded mozzarella cheese
- 1/4 cup crumbled bacon (optional)

Instructions:

1. Preheat the oven to 475°F (245°C).
2. Spread cheddar cheese sauce on the dough, then top with macaroni pasta.
3. Sprinkle with mozzarella cheese and bacon (optional).
4. Bake for 12-15 minutes, until the cheese is bubbly and golden.

Dark Chocolate and Strawberry Dessert Pizza

Ingredients:

- 1 pizza dough (sweet or regular)
- 1/2 cup dark chocolate, melted
- 1/2 cup fresh strawberries, sliced
- 1/4 cup mascarpone cheese
- 1 tbsp honey for drizzling
- Powdered sugar for dusting

Instructions:

1. Preheat the oven to 475°F (245°C).
2. Spread a thin layer of mascarpone cheese on the dough, then drizzle with melted dark chocolate.
3. Top with sliced strawberries and bake for 8-10 minutes.
4. Drizzle with honey and dust with powdered sugar before serving.